DOING
RESEARCH T

POCKET STUDY SKILLS

*Series Editor: **Kate Williams**, Oxford Brookes University, UK*

Illustrations by Sallie Godwin

For the time-pushed student, the *Pocket Study Skills* pack a lot of advice into a little book. Each guide focuses on a single crucial aspect of study giving you step-by-step guidance, handy tips and clear advice on how to approach the important areas which will continually be at the core of your studies.

Published

POCKET STUDY SKILLS

Gary Thomas

DOING RESEARCH

macmillan education

palgrave

First published 2011 by
PALGRAVE MACMILLAN

Palgrave Macmillan in the UK is an imprint of Macmillan Publishers Limited, registered in England, company number 785998, of 4 Crinan Street, London N1 9XW.

Palgrave Macmillan in the US is a division of St Martin's Press LLC, 175 Fifth Avenue, New York, NY 10010.

Palgrave Macmillan is the global academic imprint of the above companies and has companies and representatives throughout the world.

Palgrave® and Macmillan® are registered trademarks in the United States, the United Kingdom, Europe and other countries

ISBN-13: 978-0-230-29016-7

This book is printed on paper suitable for recycling and made from fully managed and sustained forest sources. Logging, pulping and manufacturing processes are expected to conform to the environmental regulations of the country of origin.

A catalogue record for this book is available from the British Library.

Printed in China

Contents

Acknowledgements

I am enormously grateful to Kate Williams, the editor of the Palgrave Pocket Study Skills series, for her idea for this book and for her invaluable advice and guidance in improving drafts. Many thanks also to colleagues and students at the University of Birmingham for their guidance and support. Huge thanks to Sallie Godwin for her excellent illustrations and to all of the editorial and production teams at Palgrave for their detailed work. Screenshots of Excel pages are used with permission from Microsoft®.

What is research?

research: *v.* investigate; study; explore; delve into; examine; inquire; seek; look into. *n.* careful search; systematic investigation aimed at increasing the store of knowledge.

We all do research every day: research is just finding something out. Go to the National Rail Enquiries website and look up the time of the train to Penzance – that's research. There's nothing difficult about research.

But when you do research at university something else is involved. The research has to be about something more significant than train times: it's about finding out something *new*. You should be curious to find out an answer. In exploring your subject you have to base your inquiry not only on the information you collect, but also on what is already known about the subject. And your inquiry has to be thorough and *balanced* – in other words, you can't just find out what you want to find out by ignoring any inconvenient facts that you uncover.

And it all has to be done in an order that lets you build from one part to the next in what I call the five steps of research:

1. Being curious & wanting to find out something new

2. Looking to see what is already known about the subject by reading around

3. Collecting evidence

4. Using your evidence to build an argument

5. Writing it up to communicate it to others

All of this, from beginning to end – from first question to reading around to conducting your own inquiries 'out in the field' – is *research*.

And why do you need this book? You need this book because students often, too often, begin by ploughing straight into interviews or questionnaires or whatever, without really being sure why they are doing them or what they are going to end up with. Good research design helps you to join the dots and end up with a meaningful piece of research: a piece of research that will get you an 'A'.

Get a piece of paper and write down:

- *An idea* – about something that interests you, or something that is important to you in your work or your studies. (Don't worry about getting it perfect at this stage. We will refine this later.) This is what you want to research into.
- *A timetable*. You don't need much on it right now, just the date you will start and the date you have to hand in your work. (We'll fill in more details later.)

This will do for now. You have started. Marvellous! You know what you want to research into and you have a time by which you have to have completed your research project.

Ideas can come from anywhere, such as …

- a topic that you have found interesting in your lectures
- an issue at work or on a placement
- an item in the news
- something you have discussed with your friends
- brainstorming with friends or family.

If none of this works, try …

- googling websites of big government departments such as education or health
- putting 'Campbell Collaboration library' into Google to find hot topics in social scientific research
- going through the alphabet to see what topics come up as you go from A to Z. For example, 'A' might give you 'Acid rain' or 'Autism' or 'Assistants in schools'; 'B' might give 'Boot camps' or 'Botulism and botox' or 'Brazil's street children' or 'Behaviour management'; C might give 'Criminal justice' and 'Clinical excellence', and so on … Try it with friends on a long journey instead of 'I-Spy'. Fun!

Your research purpose

▸ When you were coming up with an idea, you may not have realised it but you were thinking also about your research *purpose*. Why are you interested in this idea? Is it out of basic, **intrinsic** interest – in other words, do you just find this interesting *in itself*? …

▸ Or is it with some further purpose in mind? Are you perhaps doing the research with the purpose of improving your practice in some way? (I know you are doing it to get your degree, but I mean a purpose beyond that.) This is sometimes called **instrumental** research.

Write down what you think your research purpose is, and whether it is intrinsic or instrumental.

But don't get too hung up on considering your purpose. It's just useful to be aware of this when you come to think about design, which we will look at later on.

What next?

The beginning is your idea; the end is when you hand in your completed project.

So, let's fill in the path between beginning and end. Let's unpack ... the unpacking involves getting the bits out of the research package. Those bits comprise what is often called the research *design*.

The design

There is nothing magical about design. Designing research is like designing anything else – a bathroom, a kitchen or anything: there will be things that you need for whatever it is you are designing – a bath, taps, a basin. You have to decide how much you want to spend. You need to consider the space available and where the water and drains are located. You need to decide when the work is going to be done, who will help you and what you can do yourself. All of this comprises the design of the bathroom.

Designing your research is just the same. You need to think about when to start and when to end and when you have time free to work on the project. You have to decide what tools you need to do the job – tools such as questionnaires, interviews or statistics. You need to think about how you will analyse the information that you get from these tools and how you will present it. All of this is the design. All of these bits will be carefully put together by you to make the final research project.

Questions, questions

When you are told to do a *research project* at university it is rather different from when you are told to do an *essay* or an *assignment*. With the essay or assignment you are *given* a question that you have to answer, or at least a topic area to address.

But it's harder when you have to think of the question yourself. Questions, questions. There are *so* many of them. Finding one that you can reasonably answer is your first challenge.

It's important that the question is about filling a gap in knowledge. But it should also be manageable. If you fancy a steak you don't go and bite a cow. (Apologies to vegetarians. I'm one, by the way.) You buy the right-sized piece, cook it how you like it, cut it up and stick it in your mouth. The same is true of research: you can't solve all the answers of the world, so you have to choose a manageable question and answer it in a way that suits you. Let's have a look at some questions to see what might be good or bad about them as *research questions*.

Your research question ✓ or ✗

Questions	Is this a good research question?
What are the moons of Mars called?	✗ No. You can just look it up in a book. It doesn't involve new knowledge.
Why do children fail to learn to read?	✗ No. This is too wide a question. (There are probably as many answers as there are children who can't read.)
How far was the Second World War caused by the First World War?	✓ It's a big question, but it allows you to suggest an answer and find evidence to support it.

Why does Abbi seem to 'switch off' when she has to do maths?	✓ Yes. It's just Abbi that you are concerned about – not all children. So you can suggest possible answers and then seek evidence to support those possible answers.
How did the varroa mite affect the UK honeybee population in the decade 2000–2010?	✓ Yes. It's a limited timespan that you can look at in detail and data will be readily available.

I hope you can see that a research question has to be:

- about finding new knowledge
- spooific – nul loo broad
- answerable with the resources available to you
- answerable with reasoning and evidence.

Your **question** will emerge out of your **initial idea**, but the actual question will narrow down the initial idea. It will draw a border around it and enable you to focus on it. If you find it hard moving from idea to question, remember Rudyard Kipling's poem from *The Elephant's Child*:

> I keep six honest serving-men
> (They taught me all I knew);
> Their names are What and Why and When
> And How and Where and Who.

In other words, think of these questions framing your initial interest. Remember that 'what', 'when', 'where' and 'who' lead to descriptive answers, while 'why' and 'how' often lead to answers that are about explanation. Explanation is clearly trickier than description, and we'll come on to this in a moment. (See also *Getting Critical* in this series for ways of using these key questions.)

First you need a *first question* …
and then you need a *final question*

First questions develop into final questions. You hone them until they're just right. Actually, a better phrase than 'first question' is *prima facie* question. Now I can see my readers' eyes glazing over: Latin. 'Why prima facie?' I can hear you saying.

Sorry. It's nothing technical. It's just such a useful way of describing what you need to do when you start out with your question. 'Prima facie' just means 'at first look'. It's useful because in most research, and certainly in research in the social sciences, your 'first look' question changes in the course of your work. You start with your first, naïve question, right at the beginning. You then read about the topic and maybe do some initial observations and inquiries, and after all of this your question changes. So you have your first question, which I call:

- your **prima facie question**, and
- your final question, which I call … er … your **final question**.

So, the sequence is …

- Have an idea … have a prima facie question.
- Do some groundwork: read around, ask questions, do preliminary inquiries, think about the question some more, then …
- Write out your final question – this comes after you have done your groundwork, which I discuss in Part 2.

Now that you have your questions sorted out you can be a bit more precise about your schedule for doing the research. Remember that research isn't one process; it's a collection of processes knitted together and you need to do the processes in the right order.

Let's say that you have to do a 10,000-word project that counts for a double module in your university. You have from 1 January to 1 June to complete it. The first thing to say is: don't leave it all until 15 May. This would be a bad idea. Break it up and draw a timeline like this one.

	Jan	Feb	Mar	Apr	May	June
Come up with a question	▬					
Review literature and do desk research	▬▬▬▬▬	▪▪▪▪▪▪▪▪▪				
Revise question and explore method		▬▬▬ ▪▪▪▪				
Do fieldwork			▬▬▬▬▬▬▬			
Analyse findings				▬▬▬▬▬▬▬		
Write up and hand in					▬▬▬▬▬	

Notice that some of the processes overlap. Notice also that you go in and out of some processes (dotted lines), as the need arises.

6 Checklist for planning

Have you ...

	What is it? Write it down here
1 ... got a purpose?	
2 ... had an idea?	
3 ... got a prima facie question?	
4 ... drawn a timeline?	Yes or No

To get from your prima facie question to a final question you have to do some work. It's like the bulldozers clearing a building site before a new house is built. They have to clear the ground. And so do you: you have to clear the ground. You need some kit for this: a **literature review** and a **storyboard**.

The ground clearing means rethinking your initial question and doing a bit of toing and froing. It involves what is sometimes called a 'recursive design' to your research. The alternative is a linear design, which is more usual in certain of the sciences such as physics or chemistry. However, in the social sciences and the applied sciences it is typical for the research as it is being done to affect the shape of the ultimate research. As you research you find stuff out and it affects the way that you proceed.

This diagram isn't supposed to look pretty. It's supposed to look a mess. In fact, draw in your own arrows and mess it up even more. The idea I'm trying to convey is that your research changes as you proceed: you'll have new ideas and these will affect the direction and progress of your research – these are the backward arrows on the diagram. They're not 'bad' backward arrows; they're backward in the sense of letting you think again – letting you refine your initial questions.

Once you are beyond the right-hand side of the diagram, though, do try to keep on the ⟶ straight and narrow … Recursiveness has its limits. In other words, do go into your research with an open mind, knowing that you will be changing and varying, but once you have decided, be decisive and go for it.

Let's have a look in more detail at those metaphorical bulldozers, the **literature review** and the **storyboard**.

The main reason for the literature review is to find out what has already been done. This provides a raft on which you can build your research. Without the raft, it would be much more difficult to float your research.

The literature review enables you to say 'Evans and Adams have found this' or 'There's a gap here', or 'Bloggs is disagreeing with Smith; I wonder why that is', or 'Brown and Jones both say this, but it disagrees with the general scientific view', or 'public opinion is disputed by Davies, who says …' … or something else like this.

The literature review fills in the gaps in your knowledge, or, indeed, it may create some new gaps for you. It's sometimes called 'desk research' because it may also include other kinds of preliminary investigation that you can do sitting at your desk. You may, for example, wish to look at some statistics about your subject: if you were interested in the increase in the incidence of the 'superbug' MRSA you might look at the official statistics over the last 10 years to see if you could discern any kind of 'shape' in the increase – it might have accelerated, or, by contrast, slowed down in recent years.

Now, as you do your literature review, or desk research, you will almost certainly think about changing your prima facie question. This is normal; don't worry about it. In fact, it is more than normal: it is necessary. It's part of the *clearing the ground* process. It is necessary that you should revisit your question, that you should say:

> 'Oh, I hadn't thought of that', or
> 'Oh, that has already been done by Bloggs, so I won't bother', or
> 'Oh, no one has looked at this; I think I'll look at this instead.'

In other words, the literature review helps you to refine your question. The website www. engageinresearch.ac.uk (very good for scientists) gives the example that you may have had a prima facie question about the control of the pine weevil in a forestry situation. It makes the case that the literature review could help you to focus this in such a way that you restrict your final question to one that was on method of pesticide application.

When you are reading, you have to find out information quickly. Do this in the following ways:

> ▸ Use Google, Google Scholar and Google Books. With Google Scholar and Google Books you can actually find bits of the book or article that are probably the most relevant for what you want to find out.

- Speed read – don't think you have to read every word. Many academic books are not well written and it would drive you barmy to try to read and understand every word. 'Gut' articles and books by reading the abstract (in an article) or the back cover (of a book), then skim through quickly. Look for material that is relevant to your question.
- Always keep your question in mind as you do your reading, and ask: 'How does this article/book/source relate to my research question?'
- Copy and paste key bits into a Word file, recording where you found the work, the author, title and other details and the key points. Put different references in new paragraphs (see *Referencing and Understanding Plagiarism* in this series).
- When you are in a webpage, use the *Find* facility (Ctrl F) to find key words in the material you are reading.
- Always be critical of what you are reading. The person who wrote it is only human, like you or me. If it doesn't make sense, shout at it. It's the author's fault if you haven't understood, not yours, so they deserve to be shouted at (but do remember the neighbours). Try reading it once more, but if it doesn't make sense the second time, move on quickly.
- Use 'sticky notes' to highlight key pages of books and printed articles. Put the note at the place where the key text occurs on the page.

> ▶ Ask the librarian to show you how to use the most up-to-date way of accessing articles from your home computer. At the time of my writing this book it is called Shibboleth and it lets you find out almost anything you want from any article. And it's free! (Don't ever be tempted to pay good money for an article you find on a publisher's website via Google.) Actually, your university is paying for Shibboleth, and you are paying the university. So, I'll rephrase the bit about it being free: *since you are paying for it, make sure you use it*.

Once you have your information from your literature searches you need to make sense of it and to knit it into a meaningful story. One of the big problems of students' literature reviews is that they look like lists (Bloggs says x; Jones says y; Smith says z) rather than stories. Your literature review should be more like a story than a list. You should be connecting this bit with that bit, saying how this fits but that doesn't, and showing how there is a theme (or not) through the literature that you are reviewing. If, inconveniently, there is *not* a theme, say so. Suggest some reasons why this might be.

Don't be fazed by the differences in opinion that you find. Take pleasure in them, and use them to understand your field of study. As in any human endeavour there are disagreements, rivalries, conflicts, friendships and even cabals amongst the professional researchers. Try to understand why these exist: try to create a story and explain the story. Then, use your understanding to modify your initial questions. You can then progress from here.

8 Drawing storyboards

A storyboard helps you to get a mental map of the subject that you intend to study. Just to illustrate the point: suppose that you are studying Goldilocks's psychology. What was her motivation in making a visit to the three bears' house? This isn't a very clearly defined issue or question as it stands. A storyboard will enable you to think about some of the issues surrounding Goldilocks's walk.

This example shows you how easy it is to come up with fruitful avenues of inquiry on almost anything. You have a range of directions almost immediately. You could focus on the food side, looking at whether she was hungry because she was greedy or whether she was underfed. You could focus on the child welfare issues: what were her parents doing? It's surely disgraceful that a small girl should be left on her own in a forest, especially one known to be populated by bears – wait till the *Daily Mail* finds out. Or maybe she deliberately got lost: maybe she had something of a wanderlust and she had gone against her parents' strict instructions. Maybe she wasn't the paragon of virtue portrayed in all the best storybooks; maybe she was a little tearaway. We just don't know. This opens a rich vein of inquiry about Goldilocks's psychology, challenging received wisdom.

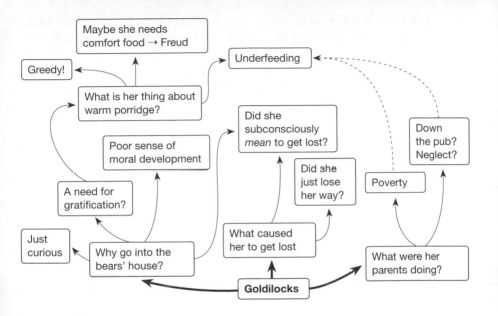

I hope you can see that even using this example we can draw into the storyboard some quite interesting potential avenues of exploration, each of them offering separate lines of questioning and separate sources of evidence towards a solution. Sadly, we know so little about the real Goldilocks: there isn't a huge amount of literature about Goldilocks's parents' income or her taste in food. But in a real example, that knowledge will exist in the literature.

So, potential lines of reasoning open up to you as you do the work. As you have been doing your literature review and drawing your storyboards you will have been thinking very hard about your research topic. You'll be able to say, 'I want to do x', or 'No, I don't want to do x any more, I want to find out about y.'

What you must now do is to establish and make clear how your argument will proceed.

The first thing to do in setting out your likely argument is to establish the problem in the ground that you have cleared. You have straightened things out a bit. Now you can be clear about where the issues lie.

Finding an angle

This is often the weakest point in student research (and, indeed, much research conducted by professional researchers and academics). I call it the 'so what?' problem … You are looking at the use of information technology in the classroom. **So what?** You are looking at how dentists use their hygienists. **So what?** You are looking at the control of vine weevils by pesticides. **So what?**

The topic has to be interesting and meaningful to the reader: it has to relate to something that conspicuously will benefit from research, so that no one can say 'So what?' Your question therefore has to be set in a context that establishes an issue or an '**angle**' on a theme. You should be in a position to do this now, because you have – with your literature review and your storyboard – got a good feel for where the issues in the field lie. An excellent book for further reading on this is *The craft of research* by Booth et al. (2003).

Once you know where the issue is you can promise a way of looking at it. You can now go back to your Introduction and explain the ultimate direction you have decided to take in your research.

1 First, you need to explain that you have established some common ground on which everyone agrees.
2 Then you have to point out that there is a problem or an issue. (Perhaps people disagree on how to deal with something that emerges from the common ground.)
3 Then you need to propose an angle from which you will address this problem or issue.
4 Then you need to promise some kind of answer.

The opening context will contain some common ground on which everyone can agree. The problem or 'angle' contains two parts: (i) some missing evidence or contradictory reasoning, and (ii) the consequences of not having an answer. The response concerns your promise of a solution.

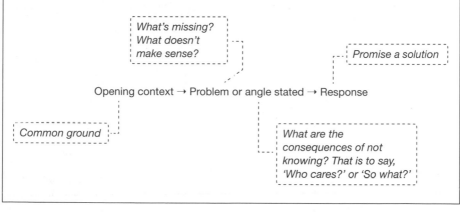

Let's have a look at this in a real-life issue: the inclusion of children with learning difficulties into ordinary schools.

General stages	Specific proposals
First, you need to establish some **common ground** on which everyone agrees.	Everyone agrees that equity and diversity are good things.
Then you have to point out that there is a **problem or an issue**. (Perhaps people disagree on how to deal with something that emerges from the common ground.) Then you need to propose an **angle** from which you will address this problem or issue. The angle may offer a frame for explaining the problem.	Some people say that these values should guide the way that we structure the school system: all children should be educated together. Others say that this is impossible. They say that children with serious difficulties cannot practicably be taught next to those with no problems. In particular, children will tend to bully those with special needs.
Then you need to **promise some kind of answer**.	I am going to look in detail at one child's inclusion in an ordinary primary school class over a period of one week. It will be a snapshot case study where I observe the behaviour of the class towards her and her reactions to this. It will contribute to the debate about the practical possibility of inclusion.

Where does this toing and froing appear in your project write-up? You will be outlining points 1 to 4 above in your Introduction chapter. Then, right at the end of your literature review, you need a section that summarises the review and revisits these questions in the light of the review, also stating your final question.

Have you …

1 … done a literature review?	What are the main themes, agreements and disagreements? Write them down here.
2 … drawn a storyboard?	What are 'stories' that emerge? Which will you follow? Jot them down here.

3 ... looked for an angle?	In two or three paragraphs summarise what the existing research is *and then say how your research will contribute to resolving an issue in it*.
4 ... reviewed your prima facie questions in the light of the literature review?	Write down your final question, relating it to the 'angle' in 3.

BUILDING A SCAFFOLD

You have to build a scaffold, or frame, to support your research. The scaffold can be one of a variety of shapes and sizes and it will be built to guide the way your research develops.

Another term for these scaffolds that shape your research is **design frames**. Let's have a look at the ones most frequently used in small-scale and undergraduate research:

▶ action research
▶ case study
▶ ethnography

- experiment
- survey.

These are all governed by different assumptions about the world and so you have to follow particular ground rules when you adopt them. I won't go into a lot of detail about these now, since there are bigger books that can explain them more fully (e.g. Thomas 2009). However, it is useful to know what they are and what they do best so that you can choose among them.

The clue's in the name. You guessed: it's about action. And research. The idea is that you are *doing* something (there's the action) and you want to do whatever it is better. So you *research* (there's the research) into it – into your practice. Clearly this is easier if you have a practice – usually in a job – to improve. For students without a relevant job it may not seem to be the most appropriate design frame. Do think about it, though, because if you are doing a part-time job, for example as a care worker in a home for old people, it may well be that there is an aspect of your work that you could use as the basis of a research project at university. Maybe Mrs Jones and two or three other residents are not joining in with the social activity that is organised for them. The action research project would begin with a prima facie question such as 'How can I change my practice in such a way that Mrs Jones's life is improved?'

The short way to describe action research is that it is like a coil: you move onwards and upwards along the coil, learning from each thing that you do before proceeding on to the next step.

... and so on

Reappraise and refine
new new question

Take action

Reappraise and refine new question

Take action

Reappraise and refine question

START with your
initial question

Take action

You'll see that the pattern is: action → reappraise → action, etc. The action you take will be something that you think may improve your practice. In the Mrs Jones example this might be taking two minutes to talk to Mrs Jones each day. The 'reappraise' element would include gathering some data (see p. 47) to assess any effect, prior to taking another action, or amending or extending the current one.

Good further reading on action research is McNiff et al. (2003).

12 Case study

Case study is a study of one thing in its entirety. You are not trying to break up the world into variables which you aim to measure independently. Rather, you are looking in detail at the whole situation.

In the following table, you can see how case study compares with another widely used design frame, the survey. You will notice that in case study the idea is to look at a large number of inter-relating features of each case, whereas with the survey you look at a small number of features of each case.

The 'case' of case study is like a container – think of your suit**case** – and the interesting thing about this is the way that your suit**case** *contains* a whole range of things. In your own suitcase this will be your flip-flops, toothbrush, camera, jeans, etc. In a piece of research it will be the context and the people and the time.

So, if you were interested in the experience of patients waiting in a doctor's waiting room, the study would be defined by an aspect of this. It might be of one room itself – or it might be a study of one person attending a waiting room. It's up to you to decide what defines 'the case' of the case study. Is it *this waiting room* as a particularly

	Case study	Survey
Investigates …	one case or a small number of cases	a large number of cases
Data collected and analysed about …	a large number of features of each case	a small number of features of each case
Study of …	naturally occurring cases where the aim is *not* to control variables	naturally occurring cases selected to maximise the sample's representativeness of a wider population
Quantification of data …	is not a priority	is a priority

Adapted from Hammersley and Gomm (2000)

interesting waiting room (because it is especially good or bad), or is it *one person's* experience in a waiting room?

If you focused on the room itself you would want to look at features such as the dimensions, the 'feel' (clinical or warm), the entrance, the pictures on the wall, etc., but you would also be wanting to assess people's experiences in the room, by, for example, interviewing them. If, by contrast, you were looking at one person's experience you might ask them to jot down all of the anxieties, doubts, reassurances that they felt as they entered and exited the room.

You can probably see from this example that there are two parts to a case study: the **subject** (that is, the case itself – the particular waiting room here), and the **object**, which is the analytical frame that the case will be illuminating – in the example here, the experience of patients in the room. How, in other words, can the subject illustrate or help you to explain patients' experience? You will have chosen this particular waiting room because it is a good example of what you hope to reveal in your study. The subject, in a sense, serves the object of the study. The case study cannot be simply a description of something: to be research (rather than just illustration) it must have an analytical purpose – an object.

Remember that you cannot generalise from a case study, since it is only one case. The aim is *not* generalisation, so don't ask your tutor 'How many do I have to do?', because the aim is to understand this **one** case in the context of the analytical frame that you have outlined.

Good further reading on case study, he said modestly, is Gary Thomas's (2011) *How to do your case study.*

'Ethnography' is from the Greek *ethnos*, meaning folk, so ethnography means 'study of folk'. The word came to be used for a new type of social inquiry early in the twentieth century – one that said that if we are studying people (as distinct from nitrogen or pulleys) we should use our own ready-made strengths as researchers, namely, that we are *people*. Yes, you are a person; I am a person. We shouldn't try to bury this fact and aim to be objective and invisible as social researchers. We should become part of the situation we are studying. The term *participant observation* is therefore sometimes used to describe the way that ethnography works. What is the toolkit of the participant observer? It involves …

Keeping a diary

Observing naturally
(not like this)

Talking naturally with others

... keeping a diary: doing ethnography involves regularly keeping notes on all that is happening

... talking naturally with others: find out from others what they think just by normal talking

... observing naturally (i.e. not like this): look to see what people are doing, and take notes.

After you have done any or all of this, your job as an ethnographic researcher is to make sense of it (see Part 5). Good examples of ethnography (sometimes called an *anthropological* approach) in social inquiry can be found in Oliver Sacks's (1996) book *An anthropologist on Mars* and the great anthropologist Clifford Geertz's article 'Deep play: notes on the Balinese cockfight' (in Geertz 1975 – and you'll also be able to find the specific article by googling *Geertz deep play*).

An experiment in everyday terms can mean simply an informal trial. I might say: 'I'm going to do a little experiment to see if the geranium likes it better on the other windowsill.' This is fine and may give me a result worth having: the geranium might indeed do better on the other windowsill.

But this isn't a very well designed experiment. To qualify scientifically, the experiment has to be a bit better thought through. It means looking at all of the possible factors (or variables) that might affect the growth of the geranium, and then changing one – and only one – of them while holding everything else constant to assess the effect of your *one* change. The vocabulary used to describe this is as follows:

- ▶ the thing being changed is the *independent variable*
- ▶ the thing that we are interested in as an <u>outcome</u> (i.e. the health of the geranium) is the *dependent variable*.

We have to have *measures* of the effects of the changes (e.g. growth in millimetres, or changes in leaf colour).

Let's look at my little experiment again in these terms …

to see if the geranium likes it better on the other windowsill

This is the dependent variable: whether the geranium 'likes it better'. We decide to measure this by (say) its growth in millimetres.

This is the independent variable: *place* – the windowsills. We would need to keep a systematic record of the places we had moved it to.

So, a scientific experiment involves this systematic changing of one variable while you control the others. Your change might be in giving a drug versus not giving it. Or it might be in giving extra tuition (versus not giving it). The comparison of the 'giving' versus the 'not giving' is usually done in professional research by using two different groups – one getting the treatment and one not. Or it might be done by subjecting one group to two different conditions.

This would be difficult (but not impossible) to do properly with the poorly geranium. We would need a goodly number – say 20 – of sickly geraniums, all of which had been on the one windowsill. We would then divide the group into two and put half on the new windowsill (perhaps facing west) while the others, which we call the *control group*, we leave on the first windowsill (which perhaps faced north).

The table shows this more clearly:

	Pre-test	Treatment	Post-test	
***Experiment group* (of sickly geraniums)**	✐ Take first measure of height	✓ move to new windowsill	✐ Take second measure of height a week later	(You hope)
***Control group* (of sickly geraniums)**	✐ Take first measure of height	✗ don't move to new windowsill	✐ Take second measure of height a week later	(Oh dear)

Note that this experiment has had a positive outcome. We can't always (or even usually) expect this.

An alternative 'real world' experiment design would be repeatedly to move the one geranium – one week on the first windowsill, then one week on the new windowsill, then back again, and so on. (This would approximate to something called a 'repeated measures' design, or 'crossover' design.) This way, the geranium is acting as its *own* control. But there would be all sorts of problems with this design such as maturation of the plant, natural light levels changing over time – in other words everything else would *not* be constant. This is one of the annoying things about experimenting with living things – geraniums or people, as distinct from pulleys and nitrogen – and why social scientists in particular have to be so careful with experimental design.

It is quite difficult to set up an experiment in undergraduate research – but not impossible. Indeed, if you are a psychology undergraduate, setting up some kind of experiment is almost certain to be part of your practical course. You will be comparing groups of people or groups of animals rather than geraniums, and because of constraints of time and money they will be fairly small groups. The significance of any differences you find will need to be assessed using a statistical test. Here you would need to look for two *non-parametric* tests: the Mann–Whitney Test and the Wilcoxon Rank-Sum Test. You'll find out how to use them in Andy Field's *Discovering statistics using SPSS* (2009).

You have heard of surveys, I'm sure. The trouble is, many people think that *survey* means the same as *research* – but it doesn't. A survey is a *type* of research frame (i.e. one of our scaffolds) in which you collect information from a number of people – the more the better. You ask them questions – perhaps in a questionnaire (face to face, or over the phone or online), or in an interview, or they may be completing some kind of diary entry (see p. 53). The data can be of all kinds. You collect the information to describe some feature of the situation in which they exist, perhaps the pets they keep, for example, or perhaps to find out about their

... er, 'tarantula' isn't on my list

attitudes. It is all completely static – in other words, these features of the situation are *not changed* in any way, as they would be in an experiment. Once you have collected these data you can look at them for anything that might be interesting and present the results statistically (see pp. 76–89).

Have you …

1 … thought what you need to do?	What question is your research answering and what kind of research will answer it?
2 … decided what your design frame is?	What is it? Write it down here.

FIELDWORK: FINDING THE DATA

Doing research at university may mean just finding something out by looking for it in a book. However, when you are asked to do *research* by your tutors you are usually being expected to find something out **empirically**. This means that you are expected to find something *original* and from *your own experience* (i.e. not a book author's experience). To do this you need to look at the world, ask people questions, keep notes. It means using your eyes and ears.

> *Data is plural of 'datum' so we say 'these data'.*

With your eyes and ears you get **data** (or information) and with these *data* you can answer your questions and support (or not) the claims you made at the beginning of your research. When data are used in support of a proposition in this way they become **evidence**. Evidence is very important in research.

The process of collecting data is sometimes called **fieldwork**. Let's look at some of the principal ways you can collect data in your fieldwork. You can collect it through:

- interviews
- diaries
- questionnaires
- observation
- official statistics.

Let's look at these and how you might use them.

A research interview is a discussion with someone else with a purpose (your purpose, not theirs) in mind. It can be more structured and formal, or less structured and completely informal. The degree of formality is reflected in the three broad types of interview that you can do:

1 **A structured interview**. Here, you have your questions written out and you go through them in order and without deviation.

2 **An unstructured interview**. This, by contrast, is completely open. Other than directing your interviewee to the topic you want to talk about, you inject very little else into the discussion. Your aim is to find out what the interviewee thinks without influencing them too much.

3 **A semi-structured interview**. This is the happy medium. You have an **interview schedule** of themes or topics that you write out on a list in front of you but beyond this there is no structure. You just make sure that you cover each of the themes that you have on your schedule.

Interview schedule

Subject	Done?
What do you think of the royal family?	✓
Does the RF contribute to our economy?	✓
Does it accentuate or diminish class consciousness?	

The semi-structured interview, the 'happy medium', is the form of interview most commonly used by researchers. It's not a straitjacket so you can deviate from it as necessary, but you make sure you get through the issues you wanted to ask about. You should feel free to modify the questions, or ask supplementary questions. The essence of a semi-structured interview is that the structure reminds you of your aims and themes, but it does not constrain you slavishly to follow a format.

Although it is usually preferred, the semi-structured interview isn't always best. If, for example, you are doing an ethnography (see p. 38) it would be better to use an unstructured interview because your aim in an ethnography is to learn from your research participants unobtrusively – or, at least, as unobtrusively as possible.

You can record the interview:
- electronically and then copy it all out afterwards (the copy is called a transcript)
- by taking notes during the interview
- by taking notes and recording electronically at the same time.

I find that recording everything and then copying it all out is time-consuming, a bit of a bore and hardly ever worth it. It's much better, in my opinion, to take notes of the important bits and back this up with an electronic copy if necessary. So, take your recorder in with you and record the interview, but don't rely on it: just use it as a back-up to fill in bits that you have missed or where you want to remind yourself of something.

Group interviews and focus groups

People behave differently in groups from when they are on their own, and if you decide to interview a group you will do so because of this difference – because of group psychology. Maybe you want to find out how a group (as distinct from individuals) would react to an imaginary event.

Often, the term '**focus group**' is used interchangeably with '**group interview**', but the two kinds of group are very different. In a simple group interview the researcher takes a lead role – and conducts the interview with the group much as a one-to-one interview would be conducted. But in a focus group the researcher is more of a *facilitator*. If you run a focus group you want to facilitate discussion among the participants, not between yourself and the participants. You assume a marginal rather than a central role.

The focus group contains eight or so participants, all with something in common (such as 'swing' voters – what they have in common is that they are all 'swingers'). It's like an unstructured interview, but with a group. Your aim is to let the *group* set the direction. Your role – as *facilitator* or *mediator* – is to stimulate discussion and make sure it stays on track. You may do this with your comments, or with **focus materials** – such as objects, photos, drawings, newspaper stories, audio or video recordings – which the group will discuss. You may choose just to take notes, or to record in audio or on video.

A diary can be more or less structured, and it can be kept by you or by your research participants. It's not an appointments diary with a little space for an entry every day. Rather, it is a record of relevant things that happen to you in the course of your research.

Things to keep in **your own research diary:**

- Thoughts and reflections
- Feelings
- Actions
- New facts you have learned
- Bits of conversations
- Views
- Interpretations

Keep your diary straight after a session in the field. The diary can be in written note form or in audio or video recording.

If you are asking someone else to keep a diary you can make it in whatever form records the kind of information you want from them. For example, here is one I used with teachers in asking them to keep a record of who was working alongside them in the classroom.

Mon	NA mornings (not Fri) (TA)	Mrs B (support service)	LM all pms (TA)
Tues			
Wed	← Mrs T (parent) →		
Thur			
Fri		← Mrs P (parent) →	

It doesn't have to be like this, of course. It can be informal and unstructured, just as your own could be. So the forms of diary are:

	Informal	Formal
1 Your own diary		
2 Another person's diary		

A questionnaire is just a set of questions.
The questions may be given:

- face to face, and read out by the interviewer, i.e. you (so this is very much like a structured interview)
- by phone
- sent to respondents for them to complete themselves: they may be sent by post or email, or may be presented online.

You may be collecting facts (such as 'How many pets do you have?') or attitudes (such as, 'Do you think the *Daily Star* should be reclassified as a comic?'). The question-naire can be used in different kinds of design frame (see p. 33–44). It can be tightly structured (as in the examples I have just given), but can also allow the opportunity for a more open-ended response if required.

Two questionnaire rules

Bear in mind these rules when drafting your questionnaire:

▶ keep it short (try to keep to one side of A4)
▶ only ask for one piece of information per question.

Kinds of questions

You can have open or closed questions. An **open question** gives free rein to the respondent to say what they want (e.g. 'Tell me what you think about President Obama's healthcare reforms').

A **closed question** has to be answered with one of the alternatives that the questioner (i.e. you) gives. Closed questions are more common in questionnaires and there is a range of ways of providing the 'closedness' of the answer:

Now, question number 542...

Yes/no questions

The clue's in the name: they have to be answered 'Yes' or 'No'.

Multiple choice questions

Here, there are two or more answers and respondents are told either to tick one box, or to tick as many boxes as they like. For example:

Which of the following news channels have you watched in the last 4 weeks (tick as many as you like)?

BBC News 24	☐
CNN	☐
Sky News	☐
Bloomberg	☐
Other	☐ *Please specify* _____
None	☐

Rank order questions

Here, your respondents (that is, people whom you are questioning) have to put items in rank order – from best to worst, or most important to least important, or most difficult to least difficult, or most beautiful to least beautiful, and so on. For example, if you were interested in the factors that were most significant for parents who had just chosen a secondary school for their child, you might ask them to rank some alternatives that you set out for them, thus:

Thinking about the choice you have just made about your child's secondary school, please look at this list of factors and rank the three which were most important for you in making your decision. Please mark 1, 2 and 3 in the relevant boxes (1 for most important, 2 for next most important, 3 for next most important).

Ease of access	☐
Reputation	☐
Exam results	☐
Quality of buildings	☐
Opinion of daughter/son	☐
Opinion after visiting	☐
School prospectus	☐
Ofsted inspectors' report	☐
Other (please elaborate)	☐ _____

Rating scale questions

The respondent will rate something (an experience, attitude, attribute, etc.) along a continuum. For example:

If you have a headache, how effective do you find these painkillers?

	Very good	Good	Not much use	Useless	Never tried it
Aspirin					
Paracetamol					
Ibuprofen					
Codeine					

The respondent will tick only one box in each row.

The Likert scale

A Likert scale (named after the psychologist Rensis Likert) can be used in any situation where belief or attitude is being measured. You ask for agreement or disagreement with a *statement* that you provide. For example:

	Strongly agree	Agree	Disagree	Strongly disagree
1 Everyone should be given another chance, no matter what their crime.				
2 Some crimes are so serious that they should always carry a prison sentence.				
3 The police should be given stronger stop and search powers.				

Questionnaires online

One of the best known online questionnaire services is SurveyMonkey, at www.survey-monkey.com. At the time of writing it lets you construct your own questionnaire free for up to 100 respondents and gives help on the construction of a questionnaire, with 24-hour online support. If you need an alternative service that lets you survey more people you will probably find that your university subscribes to one. You can ask your tutor or someone at the Computer Centre which one is used at yours.

Observation is the foundation stone of the empirical approach which I mentioned at the beginning of the chapter. It's about getting information from what we see and hear (because observation can be about hearing too) rather than what we are told is the case. We should learn – the empirical approach says – from observing the world.

In order to observe we need to watch carefully, and we can do this in some very different ways. You can either observe systematically, looking for particular kinds of behaviour, or you can observe informally, a bit like a spy.

Thus, the first, systematic, kind of observation is called **structured observation**. The second, informal, kind of observation is called **unstructured observation**.

Structured observation

With **structured observation**, you are assuming that you can split the world into bits: bits that you can count. This includes even the world of people's behaviour. So, first you have to define what these bits will be. They may be bits of action or language or behaviour. Then you have to think of some way of counting how often these bits happen. Let me give an example.

Students' drinking habits

Imagine that you are interested in student drinking habits and whether males drink more than females – and, if so, whether this is related to frequency and speed of drinking when in a bar or pub. You decide to assess actual drinking behaviour. In other words: what kinds of drinking behaviour do students actually engage in? You decide to assess this by observing how often individuals in a group of ten students, five female and five male, are actually holding their glasses at a particular moment in time. Then, *at that moment*, you will put a tick for each one holding a glass. You'll end up with a chart a bit like this:

No, just a bit... tiddly

	1 min	2 min	3 min	4 min	5 min	6 min	7 min	8 min	9 min	10 min
Emily				✓					✓	
Naz			✓							✓
Hannah								✓		✓
Josh	✓	✓			✓				✓	
Maddy		✓								
Chris							✓		✓	
Ghazala							✓			
Nico	✓	✓			✓				✓	
Sarah				✓						
Joe				✓		✓	✓			

You will end up with, for each student, a percentage of time 'drink-holding' (calculated by number of ticks divided by total number of possible ticks for each student × 100). For example, if a student obtains 3 ticks out of a possible 10 – such as Joe in the chart – then 3/10 × 100 means the student was drink-holding for 30% of the time.

There are many ways of doing structured observation, and this is just one – it's called interval recording, since you take a record (draw a tick) depending on an interval (in this case 1 minute, as if a *Ping!* is going off in your ear at each minute interval). Other kinds of structured recording can be by duration recording – measuring the overall time a behaviour is occurring (so, for example, timing with a stopwatch the actual length of time Emily is holding a glass over the ten minutes, then Naz, etc.); or frequency count recording – recording the actual number of times each person in the group picks up the glass). If you decide to use structured recording, try to work out which would be best for your research question.

Unstructured observation

With **unstructured observation** there's *no* breaking the world down into bits that you count. Unstructured observation goes naturally with ethnography (see p. 38), because ethnography is about *participant observation.* In other words, you become part of the situation you are observing, and the trick is to make the observations as naturally as possible. You:

- watch, discreetly
- interview people
- reflect on your own experiences
- keep a diary.

All of this constitutes unstructured observation and it can happen in the natural and biological sciences as well as in the social sciences. The excellent website on research method for scientists www.engageinresearch.ac.uk/ gives the example of Dian Fossey's observational work with mountain gorillas in Rwanda. What she did was rather like the work of the ethnographer doing unstructured observation – she actually became accepted by the gorillas and was able to record their behaviour in extraordinary detail. With her work she made huge contributions to the understanding of gorilla ecology, demography and social organisation.

I said at the beginning of this section that research is about empirical work – that it is about finding something out from your *own* experience, i.e. not someone else's experience. Strictly speaking, official statistics represent someone else's experience, collected and manipulated by them. However, given that they represent data rather than evidence (i.e. they are not evidence until they are offered in support of an argument), they can be treated as empirical.

You can collect statistics from a wide range of sources nowadays. And you can copy them straight into your Excel file from an online source.

Try these sources:

- For the Department for Education (DfE) statistics website, google 'DfE Research and Statistics Gateway Home'. By the time you read this, the DfE may have a new title, so be intelligent in your googling.
- If you want to do comparisons between countries, Gapminder is an excellent website which produces animated scatterplots of features of different countries, such as income per person plotted against life expectancy. Try it at http://gapminder.org/. It can be as shocking as it is fascinating.

▶ To get population pyramids from different countries, use: www.census.gov/ipc/www/idb/pyramids.html

These show bar charts of different countries' populations in different age bands and they are called pyramids because they are usually pyramid shaped. However, with richer countries and aging populations they may not be.

Used with permission from the US Census Bureau

▶ The European Social Survey offers a mine of information http://ess.nsd.uib.no/, as does OECD website at http://stats.oecd.org/source/

▶ Local social statistics on almost anything in the UK can be found at www.neighbourhood.statistics.gov.uk/dissemination/

▶ Emma Smith's website www.secondarydataanalysis.com takes you to a wide range of UK, US and international websites. (See also her book, *Using secondary data in educational and social research*: Smith 2008.)

Have you …

1 … thought about what kind of data you can collect?	What kinds of data are these? Write down the kinds here.
2 … decided the method you will use to collect data?	What is this? Write it down here.

ANALYSING THE DATA

Once you've got all your data, what do you do with them? Remember that they are only data until you have analysed them and used them intelligently. Only then will your *data* become *evidence*. So, how do you do the analysis? Your data are likely to come in one of two main forms:

▶ words
▶ numbers.

You treat different data in different ways. Let's look at each in turn.

What is sometimes called 'qualitative research' is research to do with words. When I say 'words' I mean words joined up in the way that we usually join them up in language in our everyday lives. I don't mean isolated words, counted, as you might count them, with questionnaire responses. I mean proper grown-up sentences with meanings. How do you analyse these, other than by just taking the sentences at face value and copying them out into your research report?

Most ways of analysing words are based on the **constant comparative method**. It's all you need to know. Here's what it is:

The basic recipe for constant comparative method – step by step

1 You will need: your notes, diaries, any recordings; some different coloured highlighters; a pad of A4 paper; a pen; a computer (if you prefer to work on one).
2 You first read all of your data: interview notes, diaries, notes from observations, etc.

3 With the highlighters, highlight parts that you think are important. Use different colours for different kinds of 'important'. Do this either in a word-processing file or in hard copy. You'll begin to get an impression of key ideas or subjects that are coming up again and again. You can call these your **temporary constructs**. Make a list of them.

4 Now read through the data again, using your list of temporary constructs against which to compare (this is the *constant comparative* bit). Now make up a grid with the temporary constructs in a column on the left, and – on the right – page numbers of where the temporary construct is mentioned in your data. You can make notes and observations on the grid as you do this.

5 Delete any temporary constructs that are not earning their keep. In other words, if the temporary construct is not appearing again and again, scrub it from your list.

6 Now, after your second reading, make a list of **second-order constructs** that seem to explain your data. With them you should be able to summarize the important themes in your data.

7 If you are satisfied after a final look through your data you can label these as your **themes**.

8 Think about the themes. How do they seem to be connecting together? What matches with what? Are there any unanimous areas of agreement? Are there any contradictions or paradoxes?

9 Garnish: find ways of **visually representing** your themes – think, for example, about how you could draw them in the shape of a storyboard (or something like it), as shown on page 22.

10 Place as part of your analysis chapter.

These **themes** or **categories** are the walls and shapes that you build out of your data. Your data are the bricks – the themes are what you make of them. Your job when you are using words in this way is to find the meanings that people are putting into the words. It is these meanings that you have to think about.

There are various ways in which you can draw diagrams of your themes to show how one is connected to another. I have outlined elsewhere (Thomas 2009) how this can be done with **network analysis** and **construct mapping**.

Another good way of representing verbal data is with a 'word cloud', wherein more frequently used words appear bigger. I pasted the text from the first few pages of this book into a program called *Wordle*, available at www.wordle.net. You can choose the shape of your word cloud, so you could present the cloud like this …

… or in a range of other ways: you can be as creative as you like. There's even an option for putting the cloud in alphabetical order.

Using a wordcloud can give a 'picture' of an interview.

Using your brain (in analysing documents, for example)

Sometimes – for example, if you are doing research in history – there is no special route to analysing the data which you are finding, usually from documents and books. Here, I'm afraid, the advice is simply to use your brain. The key is to find the right documents, read them carefully, and then think about them.

It's not just in historical research that documents are important. They are important across the humanities and the arts subjects and also in social science (and even natural science, sometimes). All documents are different, so it is tricky to give general advice. However, there are one or two ways in which in a digital age documents can be examined more easily than once was the case.

You can download documents quite easily now, particularly those from the

government and other big organisations. This is especially easy if the document is in Word – and even if it is in a PDF you can, after checking copyright, copy it and then paste it into Word for fine-grain interrogation.

Tips for interrogating documents

▶ To copy everything in a PDF file, press Ctrl A while in the PDF, which 'selects all'; then press Ctrl C, which copies it (to your clipboard). Then open a blank Word document and paste the whole lot into the new Word document with Ctrl V.

▶ Learn to use a scanner. If you only have a hard copy of a document, try scanning relevant parts. Most of today's scanners have optical character recognition (OCR) software. Ask the scanner to 'read' the page you need (rather than simply taking a picture of it). You can save this text into a Word file. (Make sure you check copyright restrictions first.)

▶ Use your computer to help you analyse your text, by using, for example, the Find facility (Ctrl F).

Eyeballing

Eyeballing just means looking at your numbers to see what they tell you. What do they seem to say? Are they going up or down? Are they all around one point? Are there any that seem not to fit with the others?

Your eyeball (teaming up with your brain) is your most valuable tool in dealing with numbers and you should trust it. Sometimes it seems to me that we trust statistics too much – we should rely on our common sense as well as the statistics to tell us what a range of numbers may be saying.

Explaining

The second thing to remember with numbers is that the numbers and the statistics used to analyse them serve no function in themselves. They have no intrinsic merit. They help you to analyse, but this analysis exists in order for you to explain, discuss and communicate your findings. So, remember that when you present an analysis using numbers, you will need to explain with words. Tell the reader what you want them to see in the numbers: the **statistics don't speak for themselves**.

	Mites	Ants	Arths
Set 1	132	456	206
Set 2	121	410	314

This table tells us that [bla bla bla] and indicates that [bla bla bla]. We may infer from it [bla bla bla] ...

Before we start looking at how you might actually work with numbers in order to present them, look at the table on the next page to see a brief résumé of descriptive statistics that you might use.

Presentation	Good for ...	Comment	
Column graph	▶ comparing values ▶ ranking top to bottom	This example shows number of hospital admissions for hip fractures among women in various age bands.	
Bar chart	▶ comparing values ▶ ranking top to bottom	Since it is presented 'on its side', readers don't have to turn their heads to read long labels.	
Line chart	comparing values over time	Be careful about these. Sometimes it is not correct to draw a line, i.e. there is *not* always a *link* between one value and the next. This example shows the rise in the numbers of teaching assistants (in thousands) from 1997 to 2007.	

Presentation	Good for ...	Comment	
Pie chart	comparing each value with the total value	Think about what you are using it for. For example, it's *not* worth showing just two values (like 59% female; 41% male) in a pie chart. (It's just as easy to read the numbers.)	
Scatter chart	comparing pairs of values	For a class of schoolchildren, you may be collecting data on two variables – such as age and reading age (in months).	

Using Excel

If you are using numbers in your work and you don't know how to use Microsoft® Excel, you really need to find out how to do it. Here's a very brief introduction – use it to play around either with my imaginary data, or make up your own. (The instructions given here are for PC users; if you have an Apple Mac computer you should check the instructions in your Help guide.)

1 Click on the Excel icon on your desktop (or under 'Programs' in the Start menu).

2 Enter data in individual *cells*. In my example they are 66, 45, 54, 61 and 60. These could be 5 students' marks on an essay.

3 The cells have *references* (e.g. A2, A4). You use these references to tell Excel how to do the sums.

4 Sums (or 'formulae') are also put in cells – any cell you like – and the formula must always begin with an equals sign. The formula will contain the references of the cells.

5 When you have finished the data entry and the formula, click on a spare square. When I clicked on any other cell in the spreadsheet, the answer (126) appeared in the cell.

Using descriptive statistics and drawing charts

Once you have played around a bit with Excel you will find out how much it can do. I'll show you here a very limited range that helps in the visual presentation of your analysis. I outline the nature of these in more detail elsewhere (Thomas 2009). The most important thing is to make your analysis intelligible and meaningful to the reader.

Often, when you have some basic numbers to present you can do so in the form of a table. A table is a straightforward, no-nonsense way of presenting data and may often be all that is needed.

Let's take some figures about the overseas aid which is given by some of the world's richest countries. I have taken these figures from the website of the Organization for Economic Cooperation and Development (OECD). They show the actual amount given in official development assistance (in a column headed ODA), and then this amount as a proportion of the gross domestic income of the country (headed ODA/GDI %).

	ODA $m	ODA/GDI %
Australia	2,761	0.29
Austria	1,146	0.3
Canada	4,013	0.3
Denmark	2,810	0.88
France	12,431	0.46
Germany	11,982	0.35
Ireland	1,000	0.54
Italy	3,314	0.16
Japan	9,480	0.18
Korea	816	0.1
Netherlands	6,425	0.82
New Zealand	313	0.29
Norway	4,086	1.06
Sweden	4,546	1.12
UK	11,505	0.52
USA	28,665	0.2

As a table, this is fine, but given the number of countries involved it's quite hard for a reader to see immediately which is the 'best' and which the 'worst'. It involves readers running their eyes up and down the table to find out the relationship of countries to each other.

You would, therefore, do better to translate some of the figures into a bar chart, as follows.

Bar charts

The bar chart lets you see almost immediately the relationships involved among the different countries in this example. So, use it where you think that the table, on its own, offers too much information for instant interpretation.

Here's how you do it.

1 Copy the numbers into Excel. You may be able to copy and paste direct from the PDF to Excel, but this isn't always possible. If not, you'll just have to do it by hand.

2 Now, holding down the Ctrl button, select the columns you want to draw a chart from by dragging your mouse over the whole of each range which you wish to chart. In my case here this was column A and column C.

3 Click on the *Chart Wizard* in the menu bar (or if using Excel 2007 click the 'Insert' tab and choose a chart).

4 On the left-hand side of the dialog box that appears you will see the different chart types. We want the first one: *column*. There is also a choice of subtypes on the right. I just want the bog-standard one, so I've left it as it is.

5 I don't want to change anything else, so I just press *Finish* (bottom right).

Microsoft Excel - Excel Exercise

	A	B	C	D	E	F
1		ODA $m	ODA/GDI %			
2	Australia	2761	0.29			
3	Austria	1146	0.3			
4	Canada	4013	0.3			
5	Denmark	2810	0.88			
6	France	12431	0.46			
7	Germany	11982	0.35			
8	Ireland	1000	0.54			
9	Italy	3314	0.16			
10	Japan	9480	0.18			
11	Korea	816	0.1			
12	Netherland	6425	0.82			
13	New Zeala	313	0.29			
14	Norway	4086	1.06			
15	Sweden	4546	1.12			
16	UK	11505	0.52			
17	USA	28665	0.2			
18						

6 The chart appears! Hooray!

7 I had to stretch the chart a bit so that the names of the countries all appeared. To do this I grabbed the 'handle' on the right of the chart and pulled it across until I could see the country names appear.

8 Click on the edge of the chart. Copy it (Ctrl C), and then paste it (Ctrl V) into your Word document.

But even this isn't as clear as it could be. It would be better still if we adjusted the table so that the chart showed more clearly which countries gave the highest proportions of their income to overseas development. It's easy to sort in Excel:

1 Select the whole table by dragging over it with your mouse.

2 Click 'Data' on the toolbar at the top of the page.

3 Click 'Sort' as the drop-down menu comes down.

4 Click the little arrow to the right of the 'Sort by' box, and click 'ODA/GDI %'.

5 Click OK.

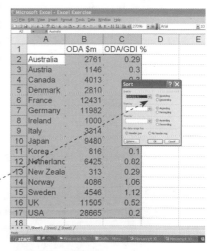

	A	B	C	D	E
1		ODA $m	ODA/GDI %		
2	Australia	2761	0.29		
3	Austria	1146	0.3		
4	Canada	4013			
5	Denmark	2810			
6	France	12431			
7	Germany	11982			
8	Ireland	1000			
9	Italy	3314			
10	Japan	9480			
11	Korea	816	0.1		
12	Netherlanc	6425	0.82		
13	New Zeala	313	0.29		
14	Norway	4086	1.06		
15	Sweden	4546	1.12		
16	UK	11505	0.52		
17	USA	28665	0.2		
18					

You can now do the same procedure as before to draw a chart. This will produce one as follows:

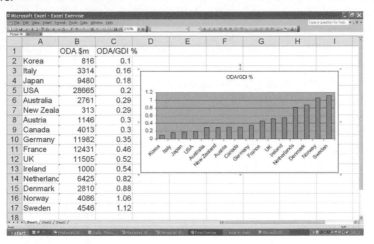

Pie charts

Where you want to show the *proportions* of the whole it may be better to use a pie chart rather than a bar chart. You do this in much the same way in Excel. Let's imagine that you want to show the top 10 languages in terms of numbers of native speakers. The figures on Wikipedia at the time of writing are as follows:

Language	Native speakers
Mandarin Chinese	845,000,000
English	335,000,000
Spanish	322,000,000
Hindi/Urdu	243,000,000
Arabic	221,000,000
Bengali	181,000,000
Portuguese	178,000,000
Russian	144,000,000
Japanese	122,000,000
German	90,300,000

To get these into a pie chart so that they can be shown in relation to one another you simply choose 'pie chart' when asked by Excel. So, following the steps as before, you:

1 Copy the numbers into Excel.
2 Holding down the Ctrl button, select the columns.

3 Click on the *Chart Wizard* in the menu bar.

4 On the left-hand side of the dialog box that appears you will see the different chart types. This time, we want the one called 'Pie' (it's the fourth one down on my copy of Excel).

5 Now, I click *Next* until I come to a step called *Chart Options*.

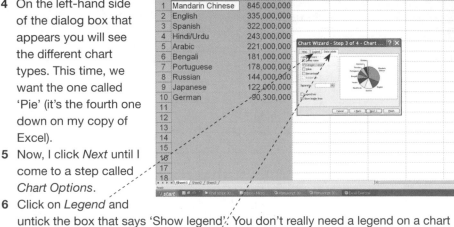

6 Click on *Legend* and untick the box that says 'Show legend'. You don't really need a legend on a chart like this. It's just confusing.

7 Now click on the tab called *Data labels* and click on *Category name.* This puts the name of each country by the relevant slice of the pie.

8 Now click *Next* until you get to the end and the chart appears.

9 Click on the edge of the chart. Copy it (Ctrl C), and then paste it (Ctrl V) into your Word document.

Other kinds of statistics

These are some of the more commonly used ways of presenting numbers visually. They are used surprisingly little by students doing research. Do remember your readers and remember that you:

▶ need to make things intelligible for them, and
▶ demonstrate to them that you can think intelligently about numbers and how they can best be presented.

So, consider how best to present your numbers meaningfully. If you explore the chart function of Excel you will find many varieties of chart that you can alternatively use.

These statistics I have described here are called descriptive statistics (because they describe) but there are of course others that have different purposes. The kind of statistic that you might use when doing an experiment is outlined on page 43. If you are using these statistics you will probably need to use SPSS rather than Excel. SPSS is available on most university pooled computers.

Have you ...

1 ... thought about what kind of analysis you need in the light of the data you have collected?	What kind of analysis is this? Write the answer down here.
2 ... decided the method you will use to analyse data?	What is this? Write it down here.

WRITING UP RESEARCH

Your reader (that is to say, your marker) will have clear expectations about what a research write-up should look like – what you should write and the order in which it should appear.

Do you remember write-ups of school science experiments? It's useful to have them at the back of your mind. You had an introduction (including your aims), and then sections which outlined the area, gave details of equipment and procedure (or methods), and then sections that dealt with results and discussion. Last, there is a conclusion. Your research write-up is similar.

All research is different so all write-ups are different. But here is a very rough summary of what might be in a typical write up:

| Chapter 1 Introduction | The introduction explains your interest in the topic of the study. At the end of it you can state your prima facie question(s) (see p. 10). |

| Chapter 2 Literature | The literature review says what other research has been done in the area. This lets you refine your prima facie research question(s). |

| Chapter 3 Method | A methodology chapter explains why you have chosen to do your research in this way. Say why you have done, for example, an action research project and a questionnaire. It's important to say *why* you have chosen these rather than simply describing them. |

| Chapter 4 Findings | Say what you actually found here. |

| Chapter 5 Analysis and discussion | Here, you analyse your findings using the tools outlined in Part 5. You will go on to discuss your analysis in the context of your research questions and in the light of any issues raised in the literature review. |

| Chapter 6 Conclusion | In the conclusion you will draw together the threads and offer the reader an assessment of how well your questions have been answered. |

Here are the rough proportions and corresponding numbers of words given to each of these sections, though I should warn you that this is only a rough guide: some write-ups will be very different. Don't feel straitjacketed by this.

Chapters	Proportion of the whole write-up (%)	Words in a 10,000-word project write-up
1 Introduction	5	500
2 Literature review	25	2500
3 Methodology	15	1500
4 Fieldwork and findings	20	2000
5 Analysis and discussion	30	3000
6 Conclusion	5	500

Just a few pages – no more

Lots of writing (but not a list, remember)

Longer than you think it needs to be – explain why you did it this way.

The guts

More guts

Just a few pages (no more)

Chapters 4 and 5 in this imaginary write-up can present a bit of a problem in knowing how best to present them. With a scientific study in chemistry or biology or certain kinds of psychology experiment you will present your chapters as neatly divided, like this. You may even separate fieldwork and findings into two separate chapters.

However, in many kinds of research in the social sciences, particularly those involving case study, it is difficult to decide how Chapters 4 and 5 should be presented. Should they be two chapters, as above, or – given the wholeness stressed by a case study – should you present these as one chapter? All the time as you are presenting your findings you will be testing them out against your thoughts and reflections – in other words, against your analysis. So all of this should be in one chapter rather than two. The difference between these kinds of study is shown here.

A research write-up in biology or chemistry, or in some psychology	Findings →	analysis →	discussion
A write-up of an ethnography or a piece of case study research in any field	Findings, analysis and discussion		

One of the questions the examiners will keep asking themselves of your research is 'Does this research address the title?' Perhaps the commonest cause of low marks is when a piece of work – research project or essay – doesn't address the title. Because of this, it is best to proceed with a working title – a provisional one – until you get to the end, and then revise this to your final title. *You* can then make sure that the work addresses the title – because it is *you* who have decided what the title is going to be. This is one of the nice things about doing research (as distinct from doing an essay) at university – you're the boss: you can decide what it is about.

It is easier to address your title if it is in two parts, with the first part giving the general context and the second part specifying more exactly the focus of your interest. For example:

> Paternalism and adversarialism in the British press:
> the influence of Beaverbrook and Rothermere on today's media

or

> Cognitive dissonance in the pre-school child: case studies of six children

An abstract comprises one – or maybe two or three – paragraphs, usually totalling 150–300 words, that give a summary of your research. It should be your research in a nutshell. In being your research in a nutshell, it should say everything that your research has been about, *including your findings*. The last bit is important, because many students leave out their findings, as if these weren't important. I have no idea why.

You should take the writing of your abstract very seriously because it is your readers' first impression of your work (and first impressions count). And your readers may, if they need reminding (as they might) of what your research is about as they read, turn back to the abstract. So, the abstract is:

▶ a summary of the project, containing a review of your …
▶ questions

- methods
- findings
- conclusions.

Write the abstract when you have finished the whole project, for the same reason that you write your title when you have finished. It's only at the end that you can decide what should be in there. Although you write it at the end, you put the abstract at the beginning, right after the title page. It is so important that it has a page all to itself.

There are some important rules for writing up research:

- Remember your reader – remember that someone is reading your work.
- Read it out loud. Does it sound right? Can *you* understand what you mean?
- Draft and edit. Then do it again. Then do it again (and so on).
- Proofread your work. Ask someone else to proofread it too.
- Number your pages. In Word, go to Insert, then Page Numbers.
- Use 35 mm (1.5 inches) margins on the left, and 25 mm (1 inch) on the right, top and bottom. Or follow your own university guidelines.
- Double-space your work, as specified by most university regulations. Select all (Ctrl A), then press Ctrl 2.
- If you quote someone else's work you must always attribute their work – otherwise it is plagiarism. If you use a quotation of 40 words or longer, indent it, without quotation marks. If shorter, keep it in the text and put quotation marks around it.
- Make sure you 'reference' work that you refer to in your write-up. All university libraries tell you how to use the Harvard method for referencing. See also *Referencing and Understanding Plagiarism* in this series.

Have you …

	✓ or ✗
1 … organized your work into chapters?	
2 … sketched out how your work will divide between the chapters?	
3 … decided, finally, on a title?	
4 … written an abstract?	
5 … got hold of your university's regulations on referencing and presentation and made sure you conform to them?	

References and further reading

Booth WC, Colomb GC, Williams JM (2003). *The craft of research*, 2nd edition. Chicago: University of Chicago Press.

Field A (2009). *Discovering statistics using SPSS*, 3rd edition. London: SAGE.

Geertz C (1975). *The interpretation of cultures*. London: Hutchinson.

Godwin J (2009). *Planning your essay*. Basingstoke: Palgrave Macmillan.

Hammersley M, Gomm R (2000). Introduction. In M Gomm, M Hammersley and P Foster (eds), *Case study method*. London: SAGE.

McNiff J, Lomax P, Whitehead J (2003). *You and your action research project*, 2nd edition. London: Routledge.

Sacks O (1996). *An anthropologist on Mars*. London: Picador.

Smith E (2008). *Using secondary data in educational and social research*. Maidenhead: Open University Press.

Thomas G (2009). *How to do your research project: a guide for students in education and applied social sciences.* London: SAGE.

Thomas G (2011). *How to do your case study.* London: SAGE.

Williams K (2009). *Getting critical*. Basingstoke: Palgrave Macmillan.

Williams K, Carroll J (2009). *Referencing and understanding plagiarism*. Basingstoke: Palgrave Macmillan.

Index